This is what you shall do: love the earth, and sun,
and animals, despise riches, give alms to every one that asks,
stand up for the stupid and crazy, devote your
income and labour - to others, hate tyrants,
argue not concerning God, have patience and indulgence
towards the people, take off your hat to nothing
known or unknown, or to any man or number of men;
go freely with powerful uneducated persons,
and with the young, and mothers of families;
read these leaves [his own works] in the open air
every season of every year of your life;
re-examine all you have been told at school or church,
or in any books, and dismiss whatever insults your own soul.

— Walt Whitman

We promise according to our hopes,
and perform according to our fears.

— La Rochefoucauld

The only way around is through.

— Robert Frost

I search in these words and find
nothing more than myself,
caught between the grapes and the thorns.

— Anne Sexton

Inspirations
Compelling Food For Thought

● ● ● ● ● ● ● ● ● ● ● ●

compiled by
Michael Ryan

0 43422 69556 0

Copyright © **1998** Great Quotations, Inc.

All rights reserved. Written permission must be secured
from the publisher to use or reproduce any part of this book,
except for brief quotations in critical reviews or articles.

Cover Illustration by Marianne Richmond
Cover Design by Roy Honegger

Published by Great Quotations Publishing Co.,
Glendale Heights, IL

Library of Congress Catalog Card Number: 95-81340

ISBN 1-56245-243-6

Printed in Hong Kong

Advice is like snow; the softer it falls,
the longer it dwells upon, and the
deeper it sinks into the mind.

— Samuel Taylor Coleridge

Here's my Golden Rule for a tarnished age.
Be fair with others, but then keep after them
until they're fair with you.

— Alan Alda

${\rm B}$eauty is an ecstasy; it is as simple as hunger.
There is really nothing to be said about it.

— W. Somerset Maugham

Use, do not abuse; neither abstinence nor excess
ever renders a man happy.

— Voltaire

You cannot acquire experience
by making experiments.
You cannot create experience.
You must undergo it.

— Albert Camus

———————————————

Never eat anything at one sitting
that you can't lift.

— Miss Piggy, puppet character

 ———————————————

Be not afraid of growing slowly,
be afraid only of standing still.

— Chinese Proverb

Choose the life which is most useful,
and habit will make it the most agreeable.

— Francis Bacon

Make happy those who are near,
and those who are far will come.

— Chinese Proverb

Here's a rule I recommend:
Never practice two vices at once.

— Tallulah Bankhead

As long as you derive inner help and comfort
from anything . . . keep it.

— Mohandas K. Gandhi

Do not invest your whole life in one hope.

— Austin O'Malley

We must learn to live together as brothers,
or perish together as fools.

— Dr. Martin Luther King, Jr.

Follow your own bent, no matter what people say.

— Karl Marx

Let him that would first move the world
first move himself.

— Socrates

God will not look you over for medals,
degrees or diplomas, but for scars.

— Elbert Hubbard

An actor is a guy who, if you ain't
talking about him, ain't listening.

— Marlon Brando

The person who wants to make it has to sweat.
There are no short cuts.
And you've got to have the guts to be hated.

— Bette Davis

Everything comes to him who
hustles while he waits.

— Thomas A. Edison

————————————

You may be disappointed if you fail,
but you are doomed if you don't try.

— Beverly Sills

 ————————————

There are only two forces that unite men - fear and interest.

— Napoleon Bonaparte

What does not destroy me, makes me strong.

— Friedrich Nietzsche

I never dared be radical when young,
for fear it would make me
conservative when old.

— Robert Frost

Art washes away from the soul
the dust of everyday life.

— Pablo Piccasso

Though we travel the world over
to find the beautiful,
we must carry it with us or we find it not.

— Ralph Waldo Emerson

The only beautiful things are the
things that do not concern us.

— Oscar Wilde

Life would be infinitely happier if
we could only be born at the age of eighty
and gradually approach eighteen.

— Mark Twain

——————————————————————————

Book lovers never go to bed alone.

— Anonymous

 ——————————————————————————

One of the greatest pieces of economic wisdom
is to know what you do not know.

— J. K. Galbraith

If you create an act, you create a habit.
If you create a habit, you create a character.
·If you create a character, you create a destiny.

— Andre Maurois

Charm is a way of getting the answer yes
without having asked any clear question.

— Albert Camus

Children have more need of
models than of critics.

— Joseph Joubert

In a great romance, each person basically
plays a part that the other really likes.

— Elizabeth Ashley

Seriousness is the only refuge of the shallow.

— Oscar Wilde

The brain is a wonderful organ;
it starts working the moment you
get up in the morning and
does not stop until you get to the office.

— Robert Frost

If this is coffee, please bring me some tea;
but if this is tea, please bring me some coffee.

— Abraham Lincoln

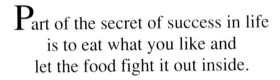

Part of the secret of success in life
is to eat what you like and
let the food fight it out inside.

— Mark Twain

$\mathbf{I}$f I had my life to live again,
I'd make the same mistakes, only sooner.

— Tallulah Bankhead

Three out of four doctors
recommend another doctor.

— Graffito

I have an existential map.
It has "You are here" written all over it.

— Steven Wright

Unsatisfied desire is in itself more desirable
than any other satisfaction.

— C. S. Lewis

Experience, which destroys innocence,
also leads one back to it.

— James Baldwin

Whathat you really value is what you miss, not what you have.

— Jorge Luis Borges

There are three ingredients in the good life;
learning, earning, and yearning.

— Christopher Morley

You will find as you look back upon your life
that the moments when you have really lived
are the moments when you have
done things in the spirit of love.

— Henry Drummond

 By all means marry; if you get a good wife,
you'll become happy; if you get a bad one,
you'll become a philosopher.

— Socrates

In the middle of difficulty lies opportunity.

— Albert Einstein

I'm opposed to millionaires, but it would be
dangerous to offer me the position.

— Mark Twain

Choose a job you love, and you will never
have to work a day in your life.

— Confucius

Each man has a choice in life:
He may approach it as a creator or critic,
a lover or hater, a giver or taker.

— Unknown

If you don't stand for something, you'll fall for anything.

— Unknown

Jack Sprat could eat no fat,
His wife could eat no lean.
A real sweet pair of neurotics.

— Jack Sharkey

Let us not look back in anger or forward in fear,
but around in awareness.

— James Thurber

$$A_n \text{ empty stomach is not}$$
a good political advisor.

— Albert Einstein

So live that you wouldn't be ashamed to sell
the family parrot to the town gossip.

— Will Rogers

Life is short. Live it up.

— Nikita S. Khrushchev

Grow antennae, not horns.

— James B. Angell

When we can't have what we love
we must love what we have.

— Roger de Bussy-Rabutin

I have never liked working.
To me, a job is an invasion of privacy.

— Danny McGoorty

We can't all be heroes because somebody has to sit on the curb and clap as they go by.

— Will Rogers

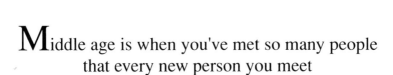

Middle age is when you've met so many people
that every new person you meet
reminds you of someone else.

— Ogden Nash

How casually and unobserved
we make all our most valued acquaintances.

— Emerson

Propaganda is the art of persuading others
of what you don't believe yourself.

— Abba Eban

Good judgement comes from experience,
and experience comes from bad judgement.

— Barry LePatner

Originality is the art of concealing your sources.

— Unknown

The human race is faced with a cruel choice:
Work or daytime television.

— Unknown

The best way to keep one's word is not to give it.

— Napoleon

Everybody likes a kidder,
but nobody lends him money.

— Arthur Miller

Don't part company with your ideals.
They are anchors in a storm.

— Arnold Glasgow

To believe your own thought,
to believe that what is true for you
in your private heart is true
for all men - that is genius.

— Ralph Waldo Emerson

The secret of life is never have an
emotion that is unbecoming.

— Oscar Wilde

$\mathbf{B}$eware so long as you live,
of judging people by appearances.

— La Fontaine

Live each season as it passes;
breathe the air, drink the drink, taste the fruit,
and resign yourself to the influences of each.

— Henry David Thoreau

If you break 100, watch your golf.
If you break 80, watch your business.

— Joey Adams

Children require guidance and sympathy
far more than instruction.

— Anne Sullivan

Freedom means choosing your burden.

— Hephzibah Menuhin

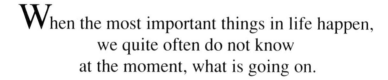

When the most important things in life happen,
we quite often do not know
at the moment, what is going on.

— C. S. Lewis

If we seek to be loved - if we expect to be loved -
this cannot be accomplished;
we will be dependent and grasping,
not genuinely loving.

— M. Scott Peck, M.D.

————————————————————————

Let me listen to me and not to them.

— Gertrude Stein

 ————————————————————————

He has the right to criticize
who has the heart to help.

— Abraham Lincoln

 I came into this world, not chiefly
to make this a good place to live in,
but to live in it, be it good or bad.

— H. D. Thoreau

A truth that's told with bad intent
beats all the lies you can invent.

— William Blake

Y̶ou are a child of the universe no less
than the trees and the stars;
you have a right to be here.
And whether or not it is clear to you,
no doubt the universe is unfolding as it should.

— Max Ehrmann

Fear makes strangers of people
who should be friends.

— Shirley McLaine

If the only tool you have is a hammer,
you tend to see every problem as a nail.

— Abraham Maslow

The art of pleasing consists in being pleased.

— William Hazlitt

There are two tragedies in life.
One is not to get your heart's desire.
The other is to get it.

— George Bernard Shaw

Life is curious when it is
reduced to its essentials.

— Jean Rhys

If our species does destroy itself,
it will be a death in the cradle -
a case of infant mortality.

— Jonathan Schell

It is good to have an end to journey towards,
but it is the journey that matters in the end.

— Ursala K. LeGuin

A house is no home unless it contains
food and fire for the mind
as well as for the body.

— Margaret Fuller

If you can imagine it, you can achieve it.
If you can dream it, you can become it.

— William Arthur Ward

Time is a dressmaker specializing in alterations.

— Faith Baldwin

Speak kindly today; when tomorrow comes
you will be in practice.

— Anonymous

Happiness is not a matter of events;
it depends upon the tides of the mind.

— Alice Meynell

We must be true inside, true to ourselves,
before we can know a truth that is outside us.

— Thomas Merton

Every great mistake has a halfway moment,
a split second when it can be
recalled and perhaps remedied.

— Pearl S. Buck

I have learned silence from the talkative;
tolerance from the intolerant and
kindness from the unkind.
I should not be ungrateful to those teachers.

— Kahlil Gibran

Our doubts are traitors, and make us lose the good we oft might win by fearing to attempt.

— William Shakespeare

Our true age can be determined by the ways
in which we allow ourselves to play.

— Louis Walsh

However much we guard against it, we tend to
shape ourselves in the image others have of us.

— Eric Hoffer

T here's a period of life when we swallow
a knowledge of ourselves and it becomes
either good or sour inside.

— Pearl Bailey

Love is when each person is more concerned
for the other than for one's self.

— David Frost

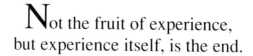

Not the fruit of experience,
but experience itself, is the end.

— Walter Pater

Keep your face to the sunshine
and you cannot see the shadow.

— Helen Keller

God creates. People rearrange.

— Joseph Casey

Everyone has a talent.
What is rare is the courage to follow
the talent to the dark place where it leads.

— Erica Jong

One faces the future with one's past.

— Pearl S. Buck

The great thing in this world is not so much
where we are, but in what direction we are moving.

— Oliver Wendell Holmes

Speak your truth quietly and clearly;
and listen to others, even to the dull
and the ignorant; they too have their story.

— Max Ehrmann

$\mathbf{B}$ut one of the attributes of love, like art,
is to bring harmony an order out of chaos.

— Molly Haskell

To love is to place our happiness
in the happiness of another.

— G. W. Von Leibnitz

Mistakes are a fact of life.
It is the response to error that counts.

— Nikki Giovanni

Always I've found resisting temptation easier than yielding - it's more practical and requires no initiative.

— Alice B. Toklas

One cannot collect all the beautiful shells
on the beach, one can collect only a few.

— Anne Morrow Lindbergh

The game of life is a game of boomerangs.
Our thoughts, deeds, and words return to us
sooner or later, with astounding accuracy.

— Florence Scovel Shinn

Once you release your expectations about the future there is only now.

— Anonymous

Eat and carouse with Bacchus, or munch dry bread with Jesus, but don't sit down without one of the gods.

— D. H. Lawrence

Every worthwhile accomplishment,
big or little, has its stages of
drudgery and triumph;
a beginning, a struggle, and a victory.

— Anonymous

 $\mathbf{W}$e should have much peace if we would
not busy ourselves with the
sayings and doings of others.

— Thomas A. Kempis

Some people are so fond of ill luck that they
will run halfway to meet it.

— Douglas William Jerrold

$$L$$ife is not always what one wants it to be,
but to make the best of it as it is,
is the only way of being happy.

— Jennie Jerome Churchill

One is happy as the result of one's own efforts.

— George Sand

I am a deeply superficial person.

— Andy Warhol

${\rm T}$radition is what you resort to when you don't have the time or the money to do it right.

— Kurt Herbert Adler

————————————————

It is better to have a permanent income
than to be fascinating.

— Oscar Wilde

 ————————————————

Assert your right to make a few mistakes.
If people can't accept your imperfections,
that's their fault.

— David M. Burns, M.D.

Stay at home in your mind.
Don't recite other people's opinions.

— Ralph Waldo Emerson

If you look at life one way,
there is always cause for alarm.

— Elizabeth Bowen

Every child is an artist.
The problem is how to remain
an artist once he grows up.

— Pablo Picasso

It seems, in fact, as though the second half
of a man's life is made up of nothing but
the habits he has accumulated
during the first half.

— Fyodor Dostoevsky

Two kinds of gratitude:
The sudden kind we feel for what we take,
the larger kind we feel for what we give.

— Edwin Arlington Robinson

An artist is a creature driven by demons.
He doesn't know why they choose him
and he's usually too busy to wonder why.

— William Faulkner

————————————————

Imagination is the eye of the soul.

— Joseph Joubert

 ————————————————

A weak mind does not accumulate
force enough to hurt itself;
stupidity often saves a man from going mad.

— Oliver Wendell Holmes

Imagine there's no country. It isn't hard to do. Nothing to kill or die for. And no religion, too.

— John Lennon

Work banishes those three great evils:
Boredom, vice, and poverty.

— Voltaire

Some people handle the truth carelessly;
others never touch it at all.

— Anonymous

There's only one corner of the universe
you can be certain of improving
and that's your own self.

— Aldous Huxley

I don't think anyone is free -
one creates one's own prison.

— Graham Sutherland

There are limits to self-indulgence,
none to self-restraint.

— Gandhi

I think somehow we learn who we really are
and then live with that decision.

— Eleanor Roosevelt

Men will wrangle for religion, write for it, fight for it, die for it, anything but live for it.

— Charles Caleb Colton

I have lived to thank God that all my prayers have not been answered.

— Jean Ingelow

Power never takes a step back -
only in the face of more power.

— Malcolm X

He disliked emotion, not because he felt lightly,
but because he felt deeply.

— John Buchan

Married couples who love each other
tell each other a thousand things without talking.

— Chinese Proverb

Nothing on earth consumes a man more completely than the passion of resentment.

— Friedrich Nietzsche

With history piling up so fast,
almost every day is the
anniversary of something awful.

— Joe Brainard

Home is not where you live
but where they understand you.

— Christian Morgenstern

——————————————

Chance makes our parents,
but choice makes our friends.

— Jacques Delille

 ——————————————

Art is a lie that makes us realize the truth.

— Pablo Picasso

Middle age is when you have a choice of
two temptations and choose the one
that will get you home earlier.

— Anonymous

It is easier to forgive an enemy
than to forgive a friend.

— William Blake

It is not what we see and touch or that
which others do for us which makes us happy;
it is that which we think and feel and do,
first for the other fellow and then for ourselves.

— Helen Keller

———————————————————

Charity and personal force are the only
investments worth anything.

— Walt Whitman

 ———————————————————

Charity begins at home, but should not end there.

— Thomas Fuller, M.D.

A good friend is my nearest relation.

— Thomas Fuller, M.D.

It is well to give when asked,
but it is better to give unasked,
through understanding.

— Kahlil Gibran

One loyal friend is worth
ten thousand relatives.

— Euripides

I have come back again to
where I belong; not an enchanted place,
but the walls are strong.

— Dorothy H. Rath

One cannot manage too many affairs.
Like pumpkins in the water,
one pops up while you try to
hold down the other.

— Chinese Proverb